How to Start a Small Business for Kids, Teens, and Young Adults Handbook

Jhinelle Walker

How 2 $tart a $mall Bu$ine$$ 4 Kid$, Teen$, and Young Adult$ Handbook

JHINELLE WALKER

"And what most people don't understand is the bulk of business in this country is small business." – Alphonso Jackson

ACKNOWLEDGEMENTS

Thanks must be given to Andrew Morrison, the CEO of the Small Business Camp, which I have attended in person and online for two years.

I thank my parents, Glenroy and Judith Walker. If it wasn't for them, I wouldn't have met Andrew Morrison in the first place. And my sister, Jhilene Walker, who was right there alongside me.

I can't forget my friends, Tiarra Spencer and Nicola Gordon, for proofreading and editing.

I also thank my church's Bishop Reyford Mott, his wife, Pastor Sherrie Mott, my aunt, Anette White, and the whole fellowship of Family Christian Center, for supporting me, along with my former middle school librarian, Concetta Mocchia, and principal, Dr. Anthony Bongo.

ISBN: 978-1-300-14731-2

Book Cover: Sihle Mnisi

Table of Contents

Introduction – Personal Note

Hello, you young, soon-to-be small business CEOs. I am Jhinelle Walker, a 14 year old, as of now, small business owner. My small business is called *Random Nation*, and it has its own blog/website, social media accounts, online store brand, podcast, newspaper, and more.

In this small handbook, I plan to advise you on how to take a simple, vague idea you have floating around in your head and help you build it in to a reality. You will be pleasantly surprised by what you can accomplish with just these few tips.

Some things you should expect when reading this are how you will be able to grasp an idea and give it a name and logo. Once you accomplish that, you will learn how to build an official website, raise funds, advertise to grow it, and connect to others. The key to having a successful business is getting known, and the best way to do that is through the Internet. So, all you need is an idea, a computer, a notepad, and a parent's supervision when it is necessary. However, if they want to participate, do not push them away. Use them.

One thing you need to know is that you can start a business from scratch, but to reach really, really far, you will need a little cash. I do not mean that you need to go rushing in with all the money you have. You only need to use it when you are ready to have more leniency and ownership online and outside.

Before I do anything else, I must give a **boat-load** of recognition and appreciation to the one man who inspired me and many others to do things like this and much more. He is the man who taught me what I am about to tell you. His name is Andrew Morrison, and he is the owner of *Small Business Camp[1]* (*Young CEO Camp*) which occurs during the summer for two weeks.

Now, we are ready to begin learning, but remember I can only teach you what I know. Whether you are successful or not depends on you. And do not forget, as a dear friend once quoted:

"Businesses always start slow."–Tiarra Spencer, my writing buddy.

-Jhinelle Walker, 16 year old CEO

P.S. – You may detect sarcasm weaved into my written text. This is a book for youth so I will speak—write like my age and relate. We have a universal language, people. Read

---

[1]   http://www.smallbusinesscamp.com/

this, and imagine a cheeky teenage girl's voice. That will add a whole new feel to it. But don't you for one second doubt my seriousness on this topic. Now, read on.

Chapter 1: An Idea

The first step in starting a small business is coming up with an idea of what it will be about or what its goals will be.

"How do I come up with an idea?" you ask.

Well, the answer to that depends on **you**. Yes, **you.** I am not talking to anyone else—metaphorically. **You** must consider **yourself** and what **you** do. What are **your** likes? Dislikes? What are **you** interested in? Do **you** have any hobbies? Any skills **you** find remarkable?

That is what you have to take in to consideration. So, what is it?

Is it computers? If so, you can repair and upgrade computers or software for others who are looking to hire.

Is it fashion? Designing is an option that will definitely be mentioned. You can open an online store and design a variety of products.

Is it writing? You can write your own books/handbooks or charge people to write transcripts for them.

Is it marketing? You can sell products you designed or possess on many different websites.

Whatever it may be, there is almost always a money making opportunity just waiting for you to find it. So, grab your Sherlock Holmes detective kit with that stereotypical magnifying glass and disposable Latex gloves and follow the clues.

My Idea(s):

_____

_____

_____

_____

Chapter 2: Give It a Name and Logo

So, you have an idea now? Great! Well, how 'bout you give it a name. It must be something catchy and easy for other people to remember. Ask close friends and family for their opinions, but don't base your views off theirs. Yours are yours and theirs are only for reflection. You must go with what you think is good, and no one should change that unless, of course, it is inappropriate, impossible/improbable, or illegal.

A very important thing that must be remembered is that you **cannot** officially *and* legally have full ownership of something if it is already trademarked by someone else or their company. To make sure you can use that name and later, hopefully, grow it in the future, you must know that it is not trademarked by someone else. A great website you can use to make sure it can be yours is the *United States Patent and Trademark Office*[2]. You will be able to see if the name is taken already, but watch out! If your name has more than one word in it, it might say taken, but it can just be one word that is truly claimed. You

---

[2]   http://www.uspto.gov/

should read carefully to see what *exactly* is trademarked there.

If the name is taken, I am sorry, but you have no choice but to just think up a new one, or you can wait until their trademark certificate runs out. In which case, you will be delaying your business's growth. And if it isn't trademarked by someone, I say, "Congratulations to you! You can use it!"

You are allowed to trademark it yourself, but you must know that it can be expensive to do so depending on whom or what you use. But if you still want to, here is a website that has a wide variety of lawyers who can file a trademark just for you alone. It is called *Trademark Ready*[3]. They specialize in trademark portfolio management, trademark prosecution services, licensing, and trademark acquisition services. It might be very useful, so you should look it up sometime when you are ready to start trademarking.

Another thing you can do for your small business is give it a fun and/or informative slogan. It is not necessary but highly recommended. A lot of large and well-know businesses have them. It is just as useful as the company's own name. You do

---

[3]   http://www.trademarkready.com/

not believe me? You want proof of how useful they are? Well then, let's play:

<u>Guess that Company</u>

"Eat Fresh!" _____

"15 Minutes Can Save You 15 Percent or More on Car Insurance"

_____

"They're Great!" _____

"I'm Loving It!" _____

"Are You in Good Hands?" _____

So, now, do you see how helpful slogans are? A short and simple slogan can help you remember an entire company's name. You do not really need one, but you might find it very useful for you and your small business in the near or distant future.

And finally, you need a logo. It is a little nifty picture that is sure to catch the eye and make anyone take a second look. An image that will peak people's interest and make them want to find out more about you and your business. When you make a logo, it must be **bold**, *eye-catching*, and, sometimes, if it is relevant, bright! Nothing dull, or else the wandering eyes will just roll over it and never think twice about the faint memory of a boring image that they had just happened to see.

You have choices. You can always make a logo yourself by using a graphic design program or drawing it yourself, which will be based on how you think it should look like. Another option is hiring or paying a professional to make it for you. It might be easier and look better, but it will cost you money, so this is an option for the creatively-stunted or bad artists. If you cannot draw, you may always ask a friend, who can draw, to do it for you. A logo can just be a picture by itself, or you can put your company name and/or on or in it. But if you really want to get a professional to do it, here's a company that will help: *LogoNerds*[4] . They can make you a logo for under $50 dollars, a fair price for some depending on your budget. Some consider them the number one choice for small businesses everywhere.

Now, once you have all that done, you have a small business. Yay! But who cares? It might as well not exist because you are probably the only one who knows about it. It is about time you made it solid and accessible to the public.

Name: _____

---

[4]   http://www.logonerds.com/

Slogan:

_____

_____

_____

_____

Chapter 3: Make a Website or Blog

By this point, your idea should be mostly finalized, but it is okay if it is not. That will give you room for change and expansion. The next ingredient in this formula is a website and/or blog.

The importance of a website or blog is that it is the online place where people can visit to find out more about your business, sign up or subscribe for what you are offering, and/or to find something interesting or entertaining to read or watch.

Building your website from scratch is a bit difficult unless you are skilled in website programming and formatting[5]. An easier way to accomplish this step, besides hiring a pro, is to use a reliable website host, but that does not mean you have to. These are websites that provide the format for you to design, alter, and add your information, but they come with a catch. They are likely to insert their brand name into your URL[6], which can be annoying because it makes the URL longer than necessary and harder for others to remember. Some require payment to remove the attached name brand and

---

[5]   HTML, javascript, PHP, etc.
[6]   http://www.yourname.example.com/

grant temporary ownership. This way is not too costly and a very fair deal.

For a blog, a well known host is *WordPress*, but there are two domains[7]. Do not confuse the two websites for each other. It's the same brand, but the .com version is for amateurs/newbies that are not that skilled in plug-ins[8] and widgets[9] and need a little structure for them to build on. It is also hosted by WordPress itself. When you are more confident and ambitious, you can eventually move on to the self-maintained .org. It may be complicated at first, but you will get the hang of it. You will need to find a host yourself, may it be an outside web host or one of the many *WordPress* hosts that are offered. They have it done for you, but you will have to pay them monthly or buy a payment plan. So, for now, we are going to focus on the beginner one, and then we will move on to the advance creation program.

So, .com is for the inexperienced who are not ready to pay for a self-maintained

---

[7]   http://www.wordpress.com/ or http://www.wordpress.org/

[8]   Able to be added to a system to give extra features or functions.

[9]   An application, or a component of an interface, that enables a user to perform a function or access a service.

WordPress, learn the setup process, the various plug-ins and widgets, and set it up themselves. This version allows you to write regular blog posts that can contain multimedia, create pages, embed *YouTube*[10] videos, upload pictures, display your *Facebook*[11] Page and/or *Twitter*[12] Feed in the sidebar, so on, and so forth.

Using this, you have your choice of themes. Some are free, and some are a charged Premium feature; you can customize either one to your own liking. You can also add widgets to the sidebar that are provided as options. However, it is limited to what is available.

The Home page will automatically be your posts/blog page, but you can later set one of your own created pages as Home[13]. If you want to learn more about creating and building your blog, go to *WordPress Learn*[14]. When it comes to your domain, their name will be in it unless you pay annually to keep it out.

Before we move on to the other version, here are three tips on growing your blog's popularity in relation to all blogs.

---

10   http://www.youtube.com/
11   http://www.facebook.com/
12   http://www.twitter.com/
13   Appearance > Themes page in the Dashboard.
14   http://www.learn.wordpress.com/

Post regularly (if you can), write interesting posts or pages, and comment on other blogs to form connections with them. Also, using Publicize on *WordPress*, you can connect your blog to many social media sites to reach out and gain followers. In fact, the majority of my blog followers are from *Twitter*. Seeing my shared post links, they read them and followed. That really surprised me. Here I was thinking a lot of fellow bloggers must like my site. That is pretty much all the advice I have for you on that topic.

And, now, we are on to the .org *WordPress*. It can be downloaded for free from the site unless you plan to use one of the *WordPress* hosts. This version gives you far more leniency than the other because it offers much more widgets and plug-in options, adding interesting and/or useful utilities. You are also allowed to use HTML codes, add website icons, drop boxes, subscribe buttons, and contact forms, but you must already own a domain name. To purchase a domain, many rely on *GoDaddy*[15] , which has a yearly fee or payment plans. You may use other sites you discover, but be sure to check if they are reliable. After all

---

[15]   http://www.godaddy.com/

that hassle, you can pretty much do what you like.

If you want your own website, there are many sites you can use that provide templates. There is one you can use for free called *Wix*[16]. The only catch[17] is that the site will put its name in your URL like many others. But it is **free**, and you can design it almost anyway you want. It can be anything from a pizza shop to an art gallery website. *Wix* allows all things from discount announcements for sales to product images.

There are many themes and colors to choose from, and you have a lot of free-will. Adding pages is possible, and you will find it easy and simple to use. If you ever get confused by anything, remember that you can always surf the Internet for help and find solutions and helpful advice there.

Blog/Website Name:

_____

Blog/Website URL:

_____

_____

---

16   http://www.wix.com/
17   There is almost always one, isn't there?

Chapter 4: Connect

Yes, yes, yes, you have a brand name, slogan, logo, and a website. So what? None of that will ever matter unless people know about your small business. Sure, you can tell all your friends and your family, but they won't be able to help you much unless they have some serious connections. You can still enlist their help. In fact, they should be the first people you go to, but when their resources run out, you'll need something else to fall back onto. That thing will be the Internet. And by Internet, I mean some SM. And by SM, I mean just that, social medias. The SM are probably the easiest way to connect to people everywhere. This is about the time the parents or guardians step in.

All people under the age of 13 (the magic age) are not supposed to have a *Facebook*, *Twitter*, or many other SM, but that does not stop many of them. Still, I recommend that you should have your parents open the account for you and/or monitor what is happening on it. There are many dangerous and untrustworthy people out there who can harm you. *Twitter* allows anyone to follow[18] you unless you block your account, monitoring the access. You

---

[18]   I call it, fondly, update stalking.

can also block your *Facebook* profile while keeping your business page public. That doesn't always work, but it's the best you can do.

If you are 13 or older, you can join these magical cyberspace connectors, but you should still ask or inform your parents. They are responsible for you and need to ensure that you are safe online.

"So, what do I need social medias for?" you ask.

Well, they are some of the best ways to share your information. You can advertise links to websites or blogs, past and upcoming events, new videos, and other interesting things that occur; they can also be useful in business. Enabling you to present your brand's name and offers, they provide different opportunities.

Now, if you are using *WordPress*, you will be provided with an option called Publicize that allows you to link your blog to the SM. Every time you write a post, the name and its short link will be posted automatically on the SM of your choice.

If you want a SM that you can use, below is a list of the most popular ones[19]. I

---

[19]   Facebook, Twitter, LinkedIn, Instagram, Tout, Vine, Tumblr, Google Plus, StumbleUpon, Reddit, Pinterest, and

am sure there are plenty more that you can stumble across on your own.

Digg[20] is a slightly different website than the others, in that you share stories. If you put one of your posts up as a story, people can read it; if it becomes a top story, you should expect to have an onslaught of viewers on your website and maybe some new followers. That is definitely something you will want to happen.

The SM that *WordPress* Publicize offers are *Facebook*, *Twitter*, *LinkedIn*[21], and *Tumblr*[22]. It also connects to *Yahoo*[23].

When you use *WordPress*, you can set like or share buttons under all your posts, pages, search results, and media that visitors can click on if you enable them[24.] You are able to add buttons yourself, but you would need to know the button's URL and icon URL.

To access Publicize, click through the Settings > Sharing page in the Dashboard.

Facebook is a SM where you can connect with your friends and post things

---

Digg.

[20]   http://www.digg.com/
[21]   http://www.linkedin.com/
[22]   http://www.tumblr.com/
[23]   http://www.yahoo.com/
[24]   Facebook, Twitter, Google Plus, LinkedIn, WordPress Press This, Tumblr, Digg, Email, Reddit, StumbleUpon, Pinterest, email, and print.

like you current status, current and future plans, photos, links, videos, etc., and you can create pages. You can make a *Facebook* business page for your small business, so it has it own official page and URL for people to access instead of your personal account if you want to keep that private. Using *Facebook* will allow you to send out pretty much any info you want to.

Twitter allows you to follow friends, businesses, actors, celebrities, and random people. It also allows them to follow you. When you follow someone, you can see their status updates when they tweet. Each tweet is limited to 140 characters, so it must be short and sweet. It's probably one of the easiest and most efficient SM to use. You aren't just limited to family, friends, friends of friends, and parts of the public; you're open to everyone.

Google Plus[25] posts can go to your circles, friends, acquaintances, and the public. It can be useful, and people can share your stuff within their circles.

LinkedIn is one of the most popular business SM. It's meant for people who are employers or employees of companies, businesses, corporations, etc. unlike *Facebook* and *Twitter*, which are for just

---

[25]   http://plus.google.com/

about anyone and anything. You can interact with other employees or owners within your area of expertise and grow strong connections. Finding some very influential people, who will be more than willing to aid you in your progression, is a huge and welcomed possibility. I use it myself, and I have quite a few connections which link me to over 280,000 people.

Tumblr is a simple website where anyone can make a blog without all the extra fuss and features. You can link your *WordPress* and your *Tumblr* blogs together. Whatever you post on *WordPress* will automatically appear on your *Tumblr* wall. It's greatly used, and people will sometimes come across certain blogs and get interested. Sometimes, they will start posting their own things.

The SM, *Reddit*[26], is very similar to *Digg*, in where it allows people to share stories through links to posts or articles. So, you can use either or both.

StumbleUpon[27] tries to find out what sort of things interest you and then introduces you to videos, web pages, or websites that hold similar content or share a common topic.

---

[26]   http://www.reddit.com/
[27]   http://www.stumbleupon.com/

And *Pinterest*[28] allows you to take photos, websites, or posts that you like and pin them together, so that you can find them all when you need them. Some people use it to plan events such as weddings, put together a collage of fashion photos, save recipes, decorate your home, or save what inspires you online.

Another option for you is *YouTube*. It is always a great idea to use it to your advantage. You don't necessarily need to put up videos of yourself, but you can create commercials using a camera or making a cartoon. You can use professional editing websites that are easy to understand or cartoon video creators, which are provided as options by YouTube's "Create[29]," and have it published straight to your account. Though those editing websites will put their name/logo at the beginning and/or ending of your video. But if you don't want their label there or if you want to edit yourself, using *Windows Movie Maker*, *Adobe Premiere*, *Sony Vegas Pro*, *Adobe After Effects*, et cetera are also advised.

ALL of these choices, options, or possibilities increase your influence online and will increase your chances of having a lot of Internet traffic on your sites which is

---

28   http://www.pinterest.com/
29   http://www.youtube.com/create/

one of your ultimate goals. Once attention is attracted to your site, whatever you are offering is seen.

"So, how do I know how much influence I have on the interconnected web?"

There is actually a way you can measure your Internet influence and compare your score to friends, family, teachers, associates, celebs, and other people you interact with. It's called *Klout*[30], and it is easy to understand. All you need to do is connect your *Klout* account to your SM. It will report your Internet reach, your influential topics, who influences you, whom you influence, and which SM you have the most influence in.

SM I joined:

_____

_____

_____

_____

_____

---

[30]   http://www.klout.com/

Chapter 5: Expand

This is completely optional and does not have to have anything to do with your business, but it can. This chapter provides information for projects that are for fun and, sometimes, can have profit. It is about time you expanded. All you fashion designers, event planners/hosts, and public speakers out there that are reading this book, you just might enjoy this chapter, because it is time for your skills to shine through. And do not forget you video editors who love making videos like me. The rest of you, follow along, and you will find out some new ways to branch out your business and get some enjoyment out of it.

The first thing that we will discuss is opening your own chain of online stores. No, I am not playing with you; it's true and easy to do.

Two online stores that are used often by others are *CafePress*[31] and *Zazzle*[32]. Both sites provide you with a template of the product you are designing and allow you to add words, pictures, shapes, and colors to decorate the product the way you would like it. One thing you should know is that both

---

[31]   http://www.cafepress.com/
[32]   http://www.zazzle.com/

options have their fair share of pros and cons.

CafePress allows you to use their clip art and/or upload your own pictures, type in various fonts, add shapes, and use different colors. Once you save a design, it is instantly up on the market, and each design can be put on a moderate variety of clothing, accessories, and gifts. When someone orders one of your products, *CafePress* will print and produce the product and then ship it to them. You will receive part of the profit once *CafePress* takes their share. The only cons are the limited amount of designs you can have in some stores and the small choice of backgrounds. Also, you will only get a shirt template when you create a design instead of mugs, bags, hats, etc. templates. But overall, it's a very useful and reliable online store site.

And next up is *Zazzle*. Like *CafePress*, you can upload your own pictures. However, there is no provided clip art, its writing font choices are limited, and you are not allowed to enlarge pictures too much, or they will not allow you to place it on the market in your store. Moreover, it takes a day or more to appear in your store when you publish it. What is good about *Zazzle* though is that they provide a wider variety of products that can be designed and sold. Products such as iPhone cases, wallets, skateboards, and more. Plus, their storage space for one store is immense.

So, you can choose one or both to use like I did. You know—branching out. And that was for you extraordinary designers and others who just want to explore additional options and see what you can accomplish.

On to the youngsters (or older-sters) who like to plan and host events, i.e. parties, picnics, concerts, and those other exciting (hopefully) occurrences. There is a site called *EventBrite*[33] where you can plan any event you would like and receive the option to allow free admission or sell tickets. So, if your band is having a concert or your small business is having a public event, this is where you go to prepare the basic information.

To the public speakers, you can now start your own podcast for your blog/website or just for outright use. If it is for your blog, you will be able to post about it or embed it on a page. You can use a lot of podcast websites like *Spreaker*[34], but you may also use *BlogTalkRadio*[35] where you can create an account, schedule episodes, and attract listeners by having them click on the

---

[33]   http://www.eventbrite.com/
[34]   http://www.spreaker.com/
[35]   http://www.blogtalkradio.com/

episode URL link. The whole broadcast is done through the phone, but you are provided an online studio where your audience can call in and where you can play audio.

Spreaker is another podcast website that is fairly popular. You can record a podcast ahead of time or broadcast live. To have live calls on *Spreaker*, you have the option to connect it with *Skype*[36].

You must remember you **can** use YouTube to your advantage, video producers. You can make commercials or videos made purely for entertainment. It will attract people to you.

Make an online newspaper! You have the ability to create one using *Paper.Li*[37]. When you start a paper, its contents are from *Twitter*, *Facebook*, *YouTube*, *RSS Feeds*, and *Google Plus*. You choose whose or what information appears. You can add any unblocked twitter account, any post that mentions a person on *Facebook*, or any *YouTube* channel. It will appear as an online version of a newspaper with all the categories of business, entertainment, sports, etc., and people can like, share, or subscribe to it.

---

[36]   http://www.skype.com/
[37]   http://www.paper.li/

One more thing you need to know if you are constructing a video or podcast is if you want to add music, you can use songs you like, but YouTube might remove the audio from your video if the owner(s) claims it.[38] So, it is also possible to use public domain or royalty free audio/music that can be found online. Just look it up. You can also come across public domain or royalty free photos, videos, and sound effects. It is handy when you want to submit a video for a contest, or something like that, and they express opposition to no copyrighted music. Use it to your advantage.

I'll Use:

_____

_____

_____

_____

---

[38]   That's copyright infringement.

Chapter 6: Advertise

Do you recall when I mentioned that friends and family should be the first people you go to? I was not joking. Just because you have the SM, it doesn't mean you don't need to collaborate with others. Friends and family are the easiest and cheapest advertisers out there.

What you can do is tell your friends about your website, and they can tell their friends whom will tell their friends. The ripple can turn in to a wave. You can also have them post it on their SM, because they may have more or different friends and followers than you.

Your parents and relatives are essential ingredients to the mix too. If they work outside of their homes, they can easily inform their colleagues and fellow coworkers whom might pass it on.

Another thing you can do is make flyers and put them around the neighborhood or order professional cards, which will most likely cost you, and give them out to people. Take some of your allies and place the cards and/or flyers around their offices for others to see.

When it comes to the SM, remember to mention your business almost daily and regularly throughout the day. Not enough to annoy the people reading but frequently enough for it to stick in their heads.

If you are 18 years old or older, you can make an account and put up advertisements on *Google AdSense*[39] which will place ads on other websites and blogs so people can see them. If they become interested, they can click on the ad and find out more about your small business.

In any video you create or any place you visit, you can always wear shirts with your logo or carry a product that you designed yourself, like a bag, hat, or hoodie. That's advertising done by yourself, and if people ask what it is or where you got it from, you can inform them about your business.

Remember, don't be limited to just my suggestions. Go out and find more and new ways to promote your brand name to the world. Maybe you can teach me a thing or two.

Advertisement Ideas:

_____

_____

---

[39]   http://www.google.com/adsense/

Chapter 7: Get Known

There is, more or less, always a chance or opportunity to get known for something helpful or spectacular.

Being helpful can be done in person or online. You can get known in your community by doing things that make people notice you and learn your name. You can make donations, do community service, host events, create contests, or just be plain helpful by offering your services for things like babysitting or errand runs[40]. You can even wear your logo while doing these things if you would like to.

Online is another way to be helpful. If people don't understand something that you know you are skilled at or knowledgeable about, help them. You can contribute or sell your services for computer repair, video-editing, product creation, or whatever else you can do. You can answer questions that people post online or give instructions. You can even make on-screen tutorials and post them on your blog, website, or *YouTube* channel. To record your screen, there are trusted software you can find online like *Jing*[41] or *CamStudio*[42].

---

[40]   Though, to be honest, these are some things you should be already doing without prompting.
[41]   http://www.techsmith.com/jing.html/

For something spectacular, you can write a book; a full length novel, short story, or a handbook. Yup, just like I am doing myself—right now. When you write a small, informational book, it should be on a topic that you know much about. You can't write a book on how to build a firewall when your expertise is in athletics and you know nothing about computers beside the basic click, type, and search knowledge. You won't just be confusing or misinforming the readers, you'll probably confuse yourself. So, write about what you do know and do it well.

If you write a book, don't give up when you are stuck or if it is taking too long. Even if it takes a few hours or a few weeks or a few months, keep moving forward. I almost gave up when I was writing this[43]. I thought it was too hard, but when I finally realized I wanted something to remind me that if you keep on going, it can happen, I can happen, I strove to finish. It **can** happen, and you can happen.

When you finish your book, have others proofread it for you and make sure that the grammar, spelling, and punctuation are correct. Boy, do I know how hard that is. You would probably have to review your

---

[42]   http://www.camstudio.org/
[43]   Still fighting the urge.

book many times, making the necessary corrections.[44] It's painful but essential.

You probably will have to self-publish your book, because those big, important publishing companies receive thousands of transcripts everyday, and yours will be just another one lost in the crowd. So, use a reliable website that you can find by searching online. The first to appear are usually the real thing but make sure you do some research on them before you hand them your work. When you find a reliable one, add the finishing touches, make a cover or have someone design one for you, and send it in. They will print and publish it for you. And don't forget to copyright your work. You don't want anyone stealing your ideas.

I'll Do:

_____

_____

_____

_____

---

[44]   I don't even want to think about how many times I had to reread and re-edit this.

Chapter 8: GoFundMe

The last but not the least thing you need to learn is how to raise funds for your small business. And I know just the site. What you need is a *GoFundMe*[45] page.

GoFundMe is a site where people can donate money to a business idea, a charity event, a cause, and a variety of other money-demanding projects.

All you need to do is make an account, or sign in with your *Facebook* account, and design it to your liking. Next, you will have to put the description of the fund-raising project, and then people can donate to it.

You will be given the option to make a Wish List, Donation Levels w/ Prizes, and a badge to put on your website, but the most important part of it all is setting a goal. That is the amount of money you plan to reach. If people donate, there is a bar that fills up partially each time and displays the amount of money raised and also the percentage out of the total goal.

You are allowed to post updates with photos or *YouTube* videos and share the page on your *Facebook*, *Twitter*, and email.

---

[45]   http://www.gofundme.com/

When you visit the page, it will tell you exactly how many people viewed it the previously, comments, and total reach.

All in all, *GoFundMe* is a great way to raise money for what you need to fund, but always remember to keep advertising it, so people will remember. It will all pay off in the end, so, don't get too frustrated when you receive nothing at first.

Good-bye!

That's—that's all I have to teach you. I'm—I'm done. *Wow*. You now have the basics to start your own small business. You can build up from that, and now, you don't need me anymore. I feel—sad and used. Well, bye then. Good luck to you all. Contact me sometime and tell me how you are doing.

You can find all my contact information on my own blog. My URL and business number are below. I would love to hear from you all. And you must remember, when you feel like giving up, don't, because that is the moment you need to push on through. You are going through a transition, and it's so much brighter on the other side, so keep on trying. You'll do something great. I believe in you. And with that, those are my almost parting words.

Blog: *Random Nation: What's What?*[46]
Number: (914) 712-8948
Email: jhinellew@gmail.com

---

[46]   http://www.randomnation1.com/

Progress:

_____

_____

_____

_____

_____

_____

_____

_____

_____

_____

_____

_____

_____

_____

_____

_____

www.ingramcontent.com/pod-product-compliance
Lightning Source LLC
Chambersburg PA
CBHW021928170526
45157CB00005B/2235

* 9 7 8 1 3 0 0 1 4 7 3 1 2 *